PET OWNER'S GUIDE TO
KITTEN
CARE & TRAINING

Andrea McHugh

RINGPRESS

ABOUT THE AUTHOR

Andrea McHugh is a cat lover whose life has been enriched over the years by rescue cats and kittens of all shapes and sizes, each of whom has had their own unique personality. She combined her love of writing with her love of cats as sub-editor on the best selling *Your Cat* magazine and as part of her work regularly attended veterinary and animal behaviour conferences, becoming fascinated by all aspects of feline care. Today she works as a freelance journalist, specialising in writing for pet publications and lives in Lincolnshire with her daughter Madeline and partner, Mark who is a self confessed 'cat-mad' vet. She also shares her home with a handsome red Persian called Rufus.

Photography: Amanda Bulbeck

Published by Ringpress Books Limited,
PO Box 8, Lydney, Gloucestershire,
GL15 4YN, United Kingdom.

First published 2000
©2000 Ringpress Books Limited. All rights reserved

ISBN 1 86054 137 2

Printed and bound in Hong Kong through Printworks International Ltd.

CONTENTS

HEALTH MATTERS 51

Daily checks; Weekly checks;
Monthly checks; Annual checks;
Vaccinations; Parasite infections;
Common health problems;
Giving medication; Coping
with cat allergies.

UNDERSTANDING YOUR KITTEN 61

How cats see; How cats hear; How cats
communicate; Common behavioural problems;
Indoor spraying and soiling; Hatred of grooming;
Refusing the cat carrier; Aggression; Destructive
behaviour; Hunting.

GROWING UP 73

The importance of neutering;
Choosing a cattery; Caring for older
cats; Saying goodbye.

1 Taking On A Kitten

Congratulations! By reading this book you are taking the first steps to learning about the care and training of your kitten, which means you are well on the way to being a responsible cat owner. Few things in the world are as beautiful or entertaining as a new kitten but, by inviting one of these enchanting creatures to share your life, you are also taking on a big responsibility. Sadly, cat charities are full of cats whose owners did not fulfil their responsibilities.

Lost or abandoned cats are the consequence of impulse buying, or failure to neuter them, which results in unwanted kittens, and the lack of proper identification which makes it difficult to reunite stray cats with their owners.

RESPONSIBILITIES OF OWNERSHIP

To be a responsible cat owner you need to:
• Understand your kitten's needs and ensure your lifestyle and budget can accommodate them.
• Register with a vet and ensure your kitten is vaccinated against disease and wormed regularly.
• Prevent unwanted litters by getting your kitten neutered when he or she is old enough.
• Provide your kitten with a well-balanced diet, opportunities for exercise and regular grooming.
• Provide the kitten with identification such as microchipping.
• Make provision for your kitten when you go away on holiday or business.

WHICH KITTEN FOR YOUR LIFESTYLE?

Introducing a kitten into your family is a really exciting time but, to ensure that everyone, including the kitten, remains happy, you should first decide which type of cat will suit your lifestyle. For example, it is pointless buying a

When you take on a kitten, you are responsible for his well-being for the rest of his life.

longhair Persian type if you have little time to spare for daily grooming. Likewise, it may be disappointing for all parties if you adopt a rescue feral cat when you would really like a home-loving, affectionate puss to cuddle.

Rescued feral cats may be happier living on a farm or in a stable yard and you may be much happier adopting a kitten that likes the company of humans. To ensure you get the right cat for your lifestyle, ask yourself the following questions:

Why do you want a cat?
Reasons may include: for personal companionship; company for

another cat; to hunt vermin; or, perhaps, to compete in cat shows. Clearly defining your reasons will help to ensure that you get the right kitten for your requirements.
Do you live in a house or flat?
If you live in a multistorey flat you may have to keep your kitten indoors, which will entail providing a clean litter tray each day, and sufficient stimulation and exercise opportunities to ensure that he remains happy and healthy.

Will the cat have access to a garden?
If so, is the garden cat-proof? Are there other cats in the neighbourhood? How do your neighbours feel about cats?

Is there a dangerous road close to your home?
The heartbreak of losing your kitten in a road traffic accident may mean you decide to restrict or supervise his access to the outdoors, or provide him with an enclosed exercise pen.

If you work, will the kitten be alone all day?
Your new kitten may become very lonely and develop behaviour problems if he is left alone all day. Consider getting two kittens to keep each other company.

Can you afford veterinary care?
Even healthy kittens need occasional trips to the vet for vaccinations and an annual check-up. Some animal charities offer assistance for emergency treatment, but find out what is available in your area before getting your kitten. You may also like to consider pet insurance to cover you against medical emergencies.

Who will care for the cat during holidays or will you need to budget for cattery fees?
If you go away for an annual holiday, or a weekend break, you must arrange for the care of your kitten. A cat-loving neighbour may be prepared to look after him in your home or you may have to pay cattery fees, so ensure your budget allows for this.

Do you have other animals?
If so, try and ensure your kitten comes from an environment where he has already encountered other cats and dogs, to minimise stress to the new member of your family.

Do you have children? Do you plan to have more?
Cat charities are full of cats that have been abandoned because a new baby has arrived in the house. It is not necessary to dispose of your cat. You should consider this carefully prior to getting a kitten. Never buy a cat just as a baby substitute until the real thing comes along.

Are you extremely houseproud?
Even the cleanest cats can shed hair and, occasionally, scratch the furniture. If this will upset you too much, consider getting a shorthair cat that moults infrequently and try to adopt a more laid-back attitude to housework!

Make sure that all members of the family are keen on owning a kitten.

Would you be able to cope if your cat had fleas?
Central heating systems mean that the flea season can last all year long. Cats who have access to outdoors are vulnerable to flea infestation and will need treatment for fleas regularly. How do you feel about this?

Do you go away frequently?
If you are a frequent traveller, consider carefully whether you can cope with a kitten. Cats like routine and can develop behaviour problems if their routines are regularly disrupted.

Do you enjoy grooming?
If you do not have much spare time, or dislike the thought of daily grooming, opt for a shorthair, low-maintenance variety of cat.

How much free time do you have?
If you have very little, think carefully about whether you can provide sufficient care and attention for your new kitten, particularly if you intend to keep him indoors. It may be better to delay your purchase until you have more time available.

By doing your homework first you will get a much better idea about which type of cat you can provide a suitable home for and which one will suit your lifestyle and temperament.

Remember:
• Longhair and semi-longhair cats are high-maintenance. They need daily grooming and enjoy their creature comforts, often developing from fairly playful kittens into very placid adult cats.
• Shorthair cats are lower-maintenance, need less grooming and are usually happy to live both indoors and outdoors.
• Oriental cats, such as Siamese,

are very intelligent but can be quite demanding of your attention.

• Deciding whether to get a male or female kitten is a matter of personal preference. The main difference between the sexes is that male cats tend to be larger.

FINDING A PEDIGREE KITTEN

Deciding whether to get a pedigree or a non-pedigree cat depends very much on personal taste and budget. Pedigree cats can be expensive to buy and you may have to travel quite a distance to find one. The benefits of buying a pedigree include the fact that you will know what the cat will look like as an adult and you will have an idea of the temperament, strengths and weaknesses of the breed. One of the advantages of buying from a reputable breeder is that you can assume your kitten has had a good start in life and comes from parents who were healthy and disease-free. The kitten should also have been correctly weaned and have had its first vaccinations before coming home with you.

With so many different breeds to choose from and hundreds of colour variations, there is certainly a pedigree breed to suit everyone's

tastes. If you are thinking of buying a pedigree cat, you could begin by visiting one of the larger cat shows where you will see many examples of each breed. Chat with breeders at the show and write to the various breed clubs requesting information, as well as reading as many books and articles about the breed as you can. You can also write to your national governing body for information leaflets on choosing and buying a kitten and for details of how to locate a specific breed.

Another source of information is FIFE, the international show/breed body, who can provide leaflets on a number of breeds. Never buy a pedigree cat without receiving a vaccination certificate, a pedigree that goes back at least four generations, a transfer of ownership form and a diet sheet.

Getting specialist advice and doing plenty of research will help to avoid costly and potentially heartbreaking mistakes.

ACQUIRING A NON-PEDIGREE KITTEN

Some people adore the good old moggie, as the non-pedigree cat is often called, and it is true that they can make wonderful family pets. Traditionally, they are

*A chinchilla Persian: Seek expert advice
before investing in a pedigree cat.*

assumed to be hardy animals and easy to care for. You should not have to travel far, or pay very much, for a non-pedigree cat. Many charities ask only for a donation, or will even give the kitten to you in return for assurances of a good home. Be prepared to answer a lot of questions about your home and lifestyle, however, as cat charities are usually very particular about the homes their kittens go to. You may also be asked to allow a home visit by a charity representative so that they can be sure the kitten is going to a safe environment. You will undoubtedly be expected to

The 'moggie' or non-pedigree is always a great favourite.

give a written undertaking that the kitten will be neutered when it is old enough.

As well as getting a kitten from one of the larger animal charities, your local newspaper will contain details of smaller, local ones and are often full of advertisements for cats and kittens needing a good home. You may also see adverts for kittens for sale on the notice-boards of local supermarkets, or at your veterinary surgery or pet shop.

When you view kittens for sale, ask as much as possible about their background and, if possible, see the parents to get an idea of how your kitten will look when fully grown. Unfortunately, there is often little history available about the cats and kittens awaiting homes in a cat charity.

SELECTING A KITTEN

The kitten you choose should look happy, healthy and lively. Pick him up by cupping one hand under his chest and use the other hand to support his rear end. Lift him gently and bring him close to your body. Now you can check the following:

Eyes: These should be clear, free of discharge, soreness or reddened eyelids. Healthy cats should show no sign of a grey-coloured third eyelid.

Nose and ears: They must be clean and free of discharge.

Coat: This should be clean and not greasy. There should not be excessive dandruff. Check for little

Hopefully, you will be able to see the kittens with their mother.

black specks, which could be evidence of fleas.

Bottom: This should be clean, with no evidence of soiling which could indicate an infection.

THE FORMATIVE EARLY WEEKS

Research into animal behaviour has shown that the first seven weeks of a kitten's life are the most formative ones in terms of his ability to socialise with humans.

Kittens kept in isolation during this period are likely to be less trusting and affectionate with humans, so try and buy a kitten from a loving family home, where he has been handled frequently, has encountered other animals and is used to things like vacuum cleaners and televisions.

If possible, arrange to see the kitten at six weeks old, with the mother and other kittens. At all

All members of the litter should be bright, alert and active.

costs avoid buying from 'battery catteries' where breeders keep the queens (females) and kittens isolated in outdoor pens.

Visit the kitten again at about 8-12 weeks old when he is fully weaned, has had his vaccinations and is ready to come home with you.

Do not take the kitten home if he hates being handled or appears sickly, unless you can get a written assurance that you can return the kitten and get a refund on your money if the kitten does not settle or is ill.

Responsible breeders will be keen to ensure their kitten goes to a good home, so do not be afraid to ask lots of questions.

2 *Your New Kitten*

Having chosen your new kitten, you will now be anxiously awaiting the day of his arrival. The earliest he can leave his mother is at eight weeks old, but choose the day carefully so that you can give him lots of attention – perhaps the start of a weekend or the beginning of a week's holiday. If you are due to go away on vacation in the following week or two, think about delaying his arrival until you return. Similarly, if there is going to be a period of upheaval in the home, such as a family party, redecorating or major building work, you might consider postponing the kitten's arrival.

MAKING PREPARATIONS

Use the weeks after you have chosen your kitten to prepare for his arrival. Begin by stocking up on the following essentials:

Kitten food: Enquire what type

Now you have chosen your kitten, you can start making preparations.

16

A cardboard box with warm bedding makes an ideal first bed.

of food your kitten is used to eating and buy the same brand.

Food and water bowls: There is a huge variety to choose from in terms of quality and price. There are plastic, china, and stainless steel types, as well as automatic feeders and even devices that encourage your cat to hunt out food using his paws to activate a release mechanism. Fun though these novelty feeders may be, it is not necessary to spend a fortune. There are probably spare dishes in your cupboard which will be ideal for your new kitten.

Flea comb and grooming brushes: Your breeder, local charity or vet will be able to recommend which combs and

There are plenty of bowls to choose from. This is a dual container for both food and water.

brushes will be most suitable for your kitten. See the separate section on grooming for more detailed advice.

Bed: You do not have to buy a special cat bed at first. A cardboard box and a blanket will be fine.

Cat carrier: This is a good investment. You will need one for your kitten to travel home in and for any subsequent trips to the vet or cattery.

Litter tray and cat litter: Some cats enjoy the privacy of a covered litter tray but a simple plastic tray will suffice, as long as it is cleaned daily.

Toys: Often the simplest toys are best. Kittens love ping-pong balls, cotton reels, bottle tops, cardboard boxes with holes in, or catnip mice attached to a length of string or elastic. Never leave kittens unsupervised to play with these, as they can become very entangled in the string and even choke themselves.

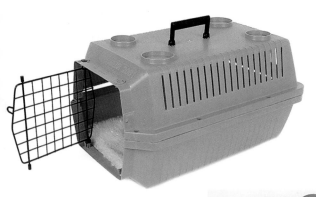

A cat carrier will be needed for trips to the vet or the cattery.

A litter tray is an essential item of equipment.

FUN AND GAMES

There is a huge variety of toys to choose from – and your kitten will love them all!

A scratching post is an essential item if you want to protect your home.

Scratching post: Cats love to sharpen their claws on a scratching post and, indeed, they need to do this to keep their claws clean, healthy and at a reasonable length. Sharpening their claws also enables your cat to leave a scent mark from his foot pads, to alert other cats that he is around. You can make a scratching post from a tree branch or by wrapping a piece of carpet round a heavy wooden post. There are also many scratching posts available to buy. Once you have positioned the post in your home, leave it in the same place, as cats do not like their regular scratching areas being moved.

Insurance: Pedigree kittens often have insurance to cover them for the first few months in their new home. Owners of non-pedigree kittens should obtain several quotes for pet insurance and opt for the one that offers most protection from unexpected vet bills. Your vet's surgery, or cat magazines, may be good sources of information on insurance.

SAFETY IN THE HOME
After stocking up on essential items, it is time to check whether your home is a safe place for an inquisitive kitten to explore. Do a quick tidy-up, storing away any favourite fragile ornaments and small items that are easily

Remember, fragile ornaments are at risk when a kitten starts exploring.

swallowed, such as elastic bands, drawing pins or sewing needles. Wrap electrical cables in tape, in particular those trailing behind your television or hi-fi, and try coating them with something your kitten will dislike, such as eucalyptus or lemon oil.

In the kitchen, ensure that cupboard doors shut properly and bottles of disinfectant and bleach are safely stored away. Kittens are attracted to the warmth of washing machines and tumble driers, so ensure all doors are kept shut and pin a warning notice nearby, reminding family members to check the machines thoroughly before turning them on.

In the bathroom, ensure that the toilet seat is kept closed, as kittens have been known to come to grief by exploring and falling in! Put a notice nearby reminding family members and friends to shut the lid. Keep all medicines and pills stored safely away in a locked cupboard and never leave a bath full of water unattended.

FINDING A VET
Register with a veterinary clinic before your kitten arrives. Vets are not only useful in times of sickness and emergency but they are excellent sources of advice on all

aspects of health care. Once you find a vet you are happy with, stick with him, as this will allow the practice to build up a complete clinical picture of your cat's health throughout his life. Word of mouth is often the best recommendation, so ask fellow cat owners which vet they see, and then pay a visit to the practice which, ideally, should be located conveniently enough for you to reach reasonably quickly in an emergency. There should also be adequate car parking. Veterinary fees vary considerably, so ask for a price list of treatments, and enquire about the possibility of paying in instalments should this become necessary.

INSURANCE

Hand-in-hand with choosing a vet is getting generous insurance against unexpected vet bills. Pet insurance is big business today and there is a wide variety of policies to choose from, with many companies offering reduced rates for non-pedigrees, who are often viewed as hardier, and therefore lower risk, than their pedigree friends. Most insurance policies provide cover against vets' bills for illness and accidents to a defined limit, and up to a certain

age, but do not cover routine vaccinations or operations such as neutering. They will not usually cover any damage the cat may cause to property in your home. Some insurance companies will offer cover for special diets and homeopathic treatments.

THE BIG DAY!

The big day has finally arrived, your preparations are complete and it is time to collect your kitten. You will need some sort of cat carrier to fetch him home in and, although cardboard ones are useful as a first carrier, they are really only suitable for short journeys. It is worth investing in a sturdy carrier with a secure lock to ensure your adult cat does not escape on future trips. Never travel in a car with a loose cat as this could be a major distraction and cause of accidents.

It is important to make your kitten's first journey as pleasant as possible, or he may associate the carrier with traumatic events, and develop a phobia about going into it the next time. Line the carrier with a thick layer of newspapers in case of accidents and pop a blanket in to give the kitten something to cling to or hide under.

Place the carrier on the front seat, having pulled the seat forward as far as it will go, and wedge the carrier against the dashboard. Now fasten the seat belt securely round the carrier, looping it through the handle. If your journey is very long, you may need to provide a litter tray and have a supply of drinking water available. Drive slowly and avoid sudden braking or turning.

WELCOME HOME

Be prepared to keep your new kitten confined to one room, with the doors and windows closed, until he settles in. Make sure you place a litter tray in one corner of the room, well away from his food and water bowls, and not in a draught. Now you can let your kitten out of his carrier!

Let him wander round the room in his own time, inspecting his

To begin with, your kitten may miss the companionship of his littermates.

new home, and then show him his litter tray and his bed, which should be away from draughts and lined with a blanket.

Your kitten will be feeling a little scared after his journey and traumatised at leaving his mother and siblings, so reassure him by talking gently and giving him plenty of cuddles. Offer him a little food and stay with him until he begins to get tired. Your new kitten will spend a lot of time sleeping; in fact, cats spend almost two-thirds of their lives snoozing. Encourage other family members, especially children, to respect the kitten's need to sleep.

Check with the breeder which vaccinations the kitten has had and collect any paperwork about this. Vaccinations are usually carried out between nine and 12 weeks and you should keep your kitten indoors for about a week after they have been done. Pedigree kittens should already have been vaccinated for cat flu and enteritis before coming home with you. More and more breeders are advocating that kittens be vaccinated against feline leukaemia as well. Allow at least 48 hours after the vaccinations before you collect your new kitten. Pedigree kittens should

also be supplied with a pedigree certificate.

A week after the vaccinations have been carried out, you may decide to allow your kitten to explore the great outdoors. You may find it easier to do this before you feed him so that he is more willing to return when called for something to eat.

Try and introduce him to your neighbours first so they know what he looks like and can return him to you if he does wander away from his own patch.

Always accompany him during his first few visits to the garden to ensure he does not get lost or frightened by anything. See the section on 'The Cat Friendly Garden' for extra tips on cat-proofing your garden.

PRETTY AS A PICTURE

It is a good idea to take photographs of your new kitten, not only because he looks so adorable but also so that you can reproduce copies of them on a poster or flier should he go missing at any time.

Take photographs of him throughout his life, as his appearance will change and his coat and markings may alter somewhat with age.

A photo will be a useful record, as well as a happy memento.

HOUSE TRAINING

Cats are naturally very clean, and most are fully house-trained when they leave their mothers, but do remember to show your new kitten where his litter tray is. Use the same kind of cat litter the kitten is used to and, each time he wakes up, take him to the tray so that he becomes accustomed to the new arrangements. Never punish your kitten if he has an accident, but be sure to clean the area thoroughly to discourage him from returning to the same spot.

Check that the cleaning product does not contain ammonia and/or chlorine, both of which are constituents of cat urine and can send out very confusing signals to a cat. Wash the soiled area with a warm solution of biological detergent and then, when the area is completely dry, scrub it with surgical spirit.

Remember to do a fabric test on your carpet or rug before you begin! See the chapter on Understanding Your Kitten for further advice on house training.

3 Family Life

There is some scientific evidence to show that children who own pets are less self-centred and more outgoing than those who do not. There is also some indication that pet ownership can increase the attention span of children with learning difficulties, and American studies of abused children reveal that pets can offer a strong supportive role during times of upheaval, such as divorce or family illness. Certainly, owning a cat can help to teach children valuable lessons in developing a sense of responsibility and respect for something other than themselves.

GROUND RULES FOR CHILDREN

Because kittens are so sweet and cuddly, very young children often find them irresistible and constantly want to pick them up and hug them. As a new owner, you must teach children that your new kitten is not a toy and cannot be squeezed, chewed or thrown about like a rag doll. Teach by example and demonstrate how to treat the kitten gently and lovingly, explaining that loud noises can be very frightening, as can sudden movements, or snatching at his ears, whiskers or tail.

Hopefully, your kitten will have experienced some family life before coming to your home, but each cat varies in personality and, while some are extremely tolerant with children, others can become impatient quite quickly. Breeders have an enormous responsibility to ensure that animals are 'bomb-proof' in the home from the start. Kittens that are already familiar with children, vacuum cleaners, loud bangs and other noises will have a far easier time adapting to your family's way of life.

From the start, establish some ground rules, teaching children not to touch your kitten while he

With careful supervision, children and kittens will be the best of friends – and playmates.

is sleeping or eating and, definitely, not to pull him by his tail. Older children can be taught to observe the cat's behaviour and apply some judgement as to whether he is contented or not. Point out that signs of displeasure include ruffling of the fur and hissing, or flattening of the ears, while signs of pleasure include purring and rubbing against the legs.

Involving children in caring for the kitten will help to develop a mutual respect between them. Asking the child to help you feed the kitten part of his daily food ration will enable the kitten to begin associating the child with positive events. Be careful not to leave uneaten cat food around for too long; apart from attracting flies, inquisitive toddlers might be tempted to sample some feline cuisine.

Good hygiene is vital, so keep the cat's food bowls and litter tray well away from children and ensure that the cat does not have access to your child's dishes. Teach children routinely to wash their hands after playing with the cat, especially before meal times.

To prevent accidents happening, keep all cat food separate from human foods, and store animal medicines such as flea powders or worming preparations in a secure place.

KITTENS AND BABIES

Whether or not you are intending to start a family should have been one of the points discussed before getting a kitten. Cats are a lifetime responsibility but, sadly, many rescue homes are full of cats that have been abandoned because they were unwanted after the arrival of a baby. One of the main concerns of pregnant women is an infection called toxoplasmosis, which can be damaging to an unborn foetus. Toxoplasma is a single-celled parasite found in almost all mammals, but cats are significant in its life-cycle.

Infected cats rarely show signs of the illness because they excrete so many of the parasites in their faeces. Other sources of toxoplasma infection to humans include handling soiled vegetables or raw meat. Your doctor or health visitor will advise you about any risks which cats pose to unborn children and the precautions you can take to guard against them.

The good news is that fastidious hygiene minimises the risk of infection. *Never* clean out a litter tray without using disposable protective gloves and a plastic apron or, even better, if you are pregnant or nursing a baby, get someone else to do this job for you, using boiling water to disinfect the tray on a daily basis. Always wash your hands thoroughly after handling the cat and wear gloves when gardening. You will also help to minimise risks by ensuring that your kitten is healthy. Veterinary check-ups, regular grooming, worming and de-fleaing, plus up-to-date vaccinations, are all necessities.

If you purchase a cat or pram net make sure you apply it carefully, stretching it tight, or your kitten may decide that the net provides a rather comfy hammock and is an ideal place for a nap. Before you close the nursery door, check that your cat is not hiding in the room, particularly if your baby is sleeping. It is important not to panic if your kitten goes near your baby – but never leave the two of them alone together. This also applies to older cats, even ones that are accustomed to babies.

Older cats can perceive the arrival of a baby in the house as threatening. This is mainly because of changes to the smells in the home and the decreased amount of personal human attention the cat receives. Be aware of this, and ensure that you

Fish-watching is a fascinating pastime for a kitten... the fish will come to no harm, as long as the tank has a secure lid.

Bird-watching is potentially more hazardous... never leave your kitten alone with unprotected livestock.

still make time for your cat. Failure to do so may result in the cat finding himself a new home where he feels he is appreciated! A cat who is used to being the centre of attention will be unhappy if he suddenly finds himself relegated to the outskirts, so you need to compensate for this by being attentive to him whenever possible, such as when the baby is taking a nap. Feline behaviour problems often have their roots in lifestyle changes such as the arrival of a baby (or even a new partner). Cats are a lifetime commitment and it is the responsibility of the owner to ensure their cats are contented and well throughout their lives.

A carrier can be used when making first introductions to the family pets.

The next step is feeding dog and kitten together. This should be built up gradually, first with the kitten in a pen or carrier.

Your kitten will soon learn to let sleeping dogs lie.

As in all households, there will be days when not everything goes to plan, but it is important not to lose your temper. Stay calm, count to ten and try not to start yelling, as neither the kitten nor the baby will understand why you are so anxious and upset!

HOUSE RULES

It is sensible to establish some no-go areas for your kitten, particularly if you have children. For example, if you never allow your kitten to enter the nursery he will soon realise this room is out of bounds. Likewise, never allow the kitten to investigate inside a cot, pram or bath, or jump up on to kitchen work surfaces. A useful tool in training your cat not to jump into, or on to, forbidden places is a plastic water spray bottle or a simple water-pistol. If the cat jumps on to the work top, immediately say a loud "No" and then aim a well-directed squirt from the water spray. Cats dislike being sprayed with water and will soon get the message that work surfaces are not attractive places to explore. Eventually, simply saying the word "No", without spraying him with water, should be sufficient. Cats also dislike the feel of aluminium foil under their paws, so covering surfaces with this will help to prevent him walking on those areas, particularly when you are not around.

KITTENS AND OTHER PETS

Successfully introducing a kitten into a multi-pet household is likely to be much quicker than with an older cat. The key to success is never to force the issue. Cats hate being forced to do anything, so rushed or poorly handled first introductions can prove disastrous.

In the wild, cats recognise newcomers by their smell. Learning to accept this smell as non-threatening is the first step to getting your older cat to accept a newcomer. You can help this process by keeping your kitten or new cat in a separate room of the house for the first day or two. This way, although the newcomer is out of sight, very subtle scent signals, unnoticed by humans, will begin to infiltrate the house. After a day or two, you can try a face-to-face introduction between the new kitten and an older cat or dog – but be very patient. The best way to do this is by using an indoor pen or large carrier. Specialist cat magazines carry advertisements for indoor pens, or you may be able to borrow one from a local breeder or charity.

The cage or carrier should be big enough to contain a bed, a litter tray, food and water. Put your new kitten or cat into the carrier and allow your other pet to wander up and sniff him. Do not worry if there is lots of hissing or growling; your kitten will be safe.

The two animals will gradually accept the fact that they can see and smell each other without threat or fear of attack. Do not leave your kitten in the pen for hours on end; short, frequent periods of introduction are most beneficial. In the meantime, keep the animals separate and give each of them plenty of individual attention. If your resident cat goes outside during the day, or your dog is out for a walk, use this time to allow your kitten to explore the rest of the house, thus distributing his scent further afield.

The next stage is to begin feeding the animals together. Feed your kitten in his pen and place a food bowl for the resident pet nearby. You can change this arrangement for the next meal so that the resident cat or dog eats his meal inside the pen and the kitten eats outside. Food helps animals to relax with each other

and reinforces the message that the new kitten is non-threatening. When the animals seem happy, you can gradually dispense with the pen, but err on the side of caution and resist the temptation to grab the kitten, or shout at the other pet, if problems arise. Being over-protective of the kitten could make your older cat jealous and could thus be counterproductive. When introducing other pets to your kitten always ensure that there are escape routes available so your kitten can hide if he needs to.

The best way to help your kitten make new friends is to take things slowly and approach introductions from the point of view of the cats rather than humans.

VENTURING OUTSIDE

When your kitten has had his vaccinations and is thoroughly settled in his new home you may decide it is time to let him explore the big world outside. This decision is entirely yours but many owners decide to confine their cats permanently to indoors, perhaps because they live near a busy road and have lost previous pets through road accidents, or other dangers such as being shot by an airgun. Some owners decide that it is unnatural and stressful to

You must decide whether your kitten is to be an 'outdoor' cat.

confine cats indoors and are happy to allow them free access to the outdoors. Certainly, there are few things more pleasurable than sitting in your garden on a summer evening watching your cat explore, perhaps by chasing leaves or climbing trees. Be guided in your decision by considering your environment, the cat's temperament and his health status.

While it is true that the outside world can contain many dangers to inquisitive kittens, there are many steps you can take to minimise those risks and still allow your kitten to enjoy life naturally as an outdoor cat.

The main danger to all cats is traffic and it is sensible to keep them indoors during peak periods, such as early morning or evening, when the roads are busiest. Outdoor cats may benefit from wearing a reflective collar, provided that this features an elastic strip which will break under tension so the cat does not strangle himself through getting caught up on something. A major disadvantage of collars is that they can be removed or lost, which is

It is important to assess potential dangers before allowing your kitten the freedom to explore.

why you should consider getting your cat microchipped. This procedure is carried out by a vet and involves the painless insertion of a tiny chip (about the size of a grain of rice) under the skin.

It is usually done in the neck area and will remain in place for the rest of the cat's life. Should the cat become lost and be picked up by the RSPCA, or taken to a vet in the case of an accident, a scanner will reveal the number of the microchip and the cat can be rapidly reunited with his owner. The cost of microchipping varies, depending on the organisation offering the service, but your vet or local RSPCA will advise you on this, and the benefits will far outweigh any costs involved. Even indoor cats can escape if a window or door is left open and microchipping offers the best chance of reuniting strays with their owners.

With time, patience, and food treats, you can teach your kitten to use a cat flap.

CAT FLAPS

Many owners allow their cats the ultimate freedom to go in and out of the house as they please by getting a cat flap fitted. Most people fit these into the back door but you could also fit one into a shed or outbuilding so the cat has access to somewhere warm and dry throughout the day. There are many cat flaps on the market, ranging from simple designs to high-tech models. Whichever type of flap you choose, ensure it is fitted about 6 inches (15 cm) from the base of the door to make it easy for the cat to step through. Place your cat flap on the side of the door which is opposite the handle as this will prevent a burglar from reaching inside and letting himself in. An electronically operated cat flap will help deter all human and feline intruders!

Training your cat or kitten to use a cat flap requires patience, but never force him through or he may decide never to use it. Instead, tempt him through with cat treats and biscuits, particularly at meal times when he is a little hungry and more likely to respond. He will soon get the

hang of it and start letting himself in and out quite happily. At least one cat I know of worked out an effective, if rather unconventional, method of using the cat flap. The door would open and his owner would observe one back leg, followed by another back leg and a tail appearing as the cat made his way in backwards! To prevent other cats from using your cat flap, consider getting a coded, magnetically operated flap that works from a magnet on the cat's collar.

You can create a cat-friendly environment in your garden.

THE CAT-FRIENDLY GARDEN

Keen gardeners can train their cat not to ruin plants by messing in borders or scratching up the flower beds. Placing marker posts in corners of the garden encourages cats to scent there, while scratching posts will help protect your favourite trees from sharp claws. Encourage cats to use one area of the garden as a toilet facility. They will appreciate a pit of dry, sharp sand on a raised area away from the reach of toddlers, especially if tall grasses are planted for privacy. Sift and top up the sand frequently. If your garden contains a children's sand pit you might consider covering this over with tarpaulin when not in use so that your cat does not mistake it for a giant litter tray.

If your garden is completely paved, you might consider planting a small grassy area, as cats are fond of nibbling grass to aid digestion. Contrary to popular belief, cats and kittens are often fascinated by water, particularly the trickles produced by smaller features such as spouting stones and pots, but keep water butts covered to prevent your kitten falling in and drowning. Ensure there are some shaded areas in the garden where your cat can escape from the heat of the day.

Cats adore plants such as catnip and cat-mint, both of which are available in seed form and are grown very easily. Care should be taken, as some plants are poisonous to cats when ingested and should be avoided. Plants purchased from a nursery or garden centre should be properly labelled. Plants poisonous to cats include azaleas, buttercups, chrysanthemums, crocus, foxglove, hyacinths, jasmine, mistletoe, morning glory, periwinkles, tulips, winter cherry and yew.

Garages and sheds are generally considered to be high-risk areas for cats and kittens but they can be irresistible for them too. One of the most toxic chemicals ingested by cats is car anti-freeze but, unfortunately, this is also tragically attractive to cats and, if swallowed, can cause irreversible renal damage. There are now safer versions available on the market which are harmless to children and pets, so check the labelling before you buy. If you suspect your kitten has eaten something poisonous, contact your vet straight away.

COMING WHEN CALLED

Teaching your cat to come when called, or at least to 'answer' you by miaowing back, is sensible, and will help you locate him quickly when he is outdoors. The best way to train him is by tapping a saucer with a fork as you shout his name. Cats are sensitive to high-pitched sounds and will hear this noise from quite a long distance.

Rattling a box of biscuits is another way to encourage your cat to return when called. You will increase the chances of him returning to you immediately if you always let him out before feeding so he is quite hungry and the sound of the biscuits will remind him to come home. Always offer your cat a food reward for coming to you when called and encourage him with lots of praise.

CAT RUNS
Many owners compromise about allowing their cats totally free access to outdoors by providing them with a purpose-built cat house with panels for runs. Many specialist companies supply these, and most advertise in cat-care magazines, or you can contact a local building company or carpenter for a custom-built design. It is worth contacting your local council's planning department prior to erecting the run and checking whether you need to obtain planning and/or building permission.

CAT HARNESSES
Some cats will happily stroll around the garden wearing a harness and lead. Not all cats will allow this, but a kitten that is accustomed to wearing a harness around the house will be more likely to accept this than an older cat. Oriental types such as Siamese seem particularly amenable to being restrained in this way. Allow your kitten to sniff the harness thoroughly before you attempt to put it on so that he becomes familiar with its smell and does not perceive it as threatening.

Wearing the harness for a few minutes, two to three times each day, and receiving constant praise and treats, will help to reinforce the idea that the harness is associated with pleasurable things. When the harness is accepted, you can try attaching the lead and letting the kitten get used to the weight of this. Walking calmly on the lead should be encouraged by treats and praise but not all cats will accept a harness and, if it causes him distress, you may have to abandon the idea.

Accustom your kitten to the harness for a few minutes each day.

MISSING KITTENS

In the unfortunate event that you lose your kitten you should:

• Enlist the help of friends and family and make a thorough search of the area, including sheds and abandoned buildings.

• Telephone local vets to see if a cat of your description has been brought in, or found injured.

• Make a flier, complete with a photograph of the cat and details of where and when he went missing. Distribute these through letterboxes in your area.

• Pin notices to trees.

• Put an advertisement in your local paper and on the noticeboards of local shops and supermarkets.

The indoor cat must be provided with exercise and stimulation to make up for his lack of freedom.

• Telephone local and national charities.

• If your cat has been microchipped, telephone the relevant organisation to alert it to the fact that your pet is missing.

• Search the same area repeatedly as a lost cat can take some weeks to establish himself in a new area.

INDOOR CATS

If you decide to confine your cat permanently indoors, you must be willing to provide him with sufficient exercise and stimulation to compensate for his lack of freedom. Failure to do so could result in unnecessary stress and destructive behaviour problems such as clawing at furniture or soiling in inappropriate places.

Owners who work all day should seriously consider getting two kittens to provide each other with company and entertainment and keep them out of mischief.

Ensure that your cat has plenty of opportunity to climb, play, explore, sunbathe and do all the things that outdoor cats take for granted.

Scratch posts are essential and climbing frames useful to protect your furniture from wear and tear. Daily vacuuming to rid your house of cat hairs, plus regular attention to cat litter trays, are all extra work but, to many owners, the peace of mind gained by keeping their cats safely indoors makes these extra chores worthwhile.

4 *Kitten Care*

Once your kitten has settled into his new home, your main task is to care for him, providing the correct diet, exercise and grooming as he grows into adulthood.

KITTEN DIET

Kittens at eight weeks of age will need four small meals per day of kitten food. Adult cat food can be very rich and cause digestive problems such as diarrhoea, so offer a good-quality kitten food. Kitten foods are high in energy to promote adequate health and growth and their texture makes them easier for kittens to manage. A heaped teaspoonful, or level dessertspoonful, of wet kitten food will be adequate at first, but kittens grow extraordinarily fast and have very high energy requirements, so he will soon require more. If he cries, offer larger portions but be careful not to overfeed tiny kittens as this can cause some digestive upset.

Your kitten may return to uneaten food but do not leave this lying around too long, especially in warm weather, as it can quickly deteriorate and begin to attract flies. One way of overcoming this problem is to feed a complete dry kitten food which you can leave down for him to eat as he pleases without the risk of it deteriorating. If you do feed dry food, it is vital to ensure that fresh water is available at all times. Your kitten will also need two small saucers of diluted milk per day, but be careful, as some kittens find cow's milk too rich, which can cause diarrhoea. Specially prepared powdered kitten milk is available from pet shops and may be more suitable.

Stick to a routine when feeding your kitten and space the meals out evenly throughout the day. Suggested times are between 6-8am, 1pm, 6pm and 10pm. A

Stick to a routine when feeding your kitten.

midday meal is essential for a growing kitten, so if you are not able to get home to feed him, try and arrange for a neighbour or friend to pop in to do it. Continue to feed four meals a day until the kitten is six months old, when you can gradually reduce feeds to twice daily by omitting the midday meal and the late evening one, although you might like to replace this with a bedtime drink.

ADULT DIET

Adult cats require fewer calories, as their growth rate slows and their energy requirements reduce, particularly after neutering. This may be a time to switch to a food with a lower energy concentrate, particularly with dry foods that tend to contain more calories. 'Light' or 'low-calorie' foods are available in both dry and moist forms and will help to prevent cats from suffering obesity. Cats evolved as hunters and are designed to eat a meat-based diet. Unlike other species such as dogs, cats do not thrive on vegetable-based diets as they are unable to synthesise the substances they need if deprived of meat. Cats have very specific nutritional requirements and, in particular, their diet must contain the amino acid taurine. By feeding a commercially-prepared cat food you will ensure your kitten is getting all the nutrients he needs for a healthy life.

FADDY FEEDERS

While cats may enjoy a treat of an occasional piece of cooked fish or chicken, feeding these regularly may encourage him to become a faddy eater. If you do feed a fresh food diet, your vet may advise you to feed extra minerals and vitamin supplements. Supplements are not so necessary if you are feeding a complete cat food, as they can unbalance the diet. Excesses of vitamins A and D can cause serious health problems as the cat is unable to excrete these harmlessly from the body.

To be certain that the food you are feeding is balanced, check the labelling. By law all pet food manufacturers must state if the

*Cat's drink small quantities of water –
but make sure a supply is always available.*

food is complete or complementary. A complete food contains everything your cat needs in the correct proportions and you need feed nothing else except fresh water. You will need to feed additional food to complementary cat foods in order to achieve a balanced diet. Your vet will be able to provide dietary advice if you are in any doubt and should always be consulted prior to changing your cat's diet or starting any supplements.

If your cat suffers from diarrhoea or vomiting, your vet may recommend a bland diet as a way of controlling his symptoms. This may be based upon white meat or fish, together with white rice, and the immediate removal of cow's milk from the diet.

DESERT CATS

The domestic cat is descended from the African Wild Cat which evolved in a semi-desert country such as Egypt. It is thought that this may be why cats have learned to adapt to hot climates and are so good at conserving body fluids. These special adaptations include not having any sweat glands, except on the underside of the paws, as well as highly efficient kidneys with comparatively

minimal urine production. Cats can also teach us quite a lot about conserving energy and preventing overheating. They are generally inactive during the hottest part of the day and will seek out shaded areas to sleep in, hunting in the early morning or evenings when the sun is at its lowest.

Moist cat food contains a high proportion of water so do not worry if your cat appears disinterested in drinking water, simply ensure that he has it available should he need it and change the water regularly. It is very important to provide cats fed on dry foods with a constant supply of fresh water.

Some cats are attracted to dripping taps and, much to the amusement of their owners, will go to great lengths to position themselves underneath one to catch any falling drops. Other cats prefer drinking from puddles or streams and many cats who will not drink tap water will be attracted to bottled mineral water. If you are worried that your cat is dehydrated, perhaps because he was accidentally shut in a hot conservatory or shed without access to water, seek immediate veterinary advice. Signs of dehydration range from weakness and lethargy, intense thirst, sunken eyes, dry gums and no elasticity in the skin to a lack of co-ordination and collapse.

EXERCISE AND PLAY TIME

Healthy, happy kittens love to play, especially games that simulate their hunting instincts, but be careful that play does not become too rough. Even a small kitten's claws and teeth can accidentally draw blood, so stop the game and say "No" immediately when play becomes too boisterous. Remember that behaviour which is charming and fun in a kitten can develop into real problem behaviour in a full-grown adult cat. Fishing-pole type toys are very popular with cats and you can either purchase these from pet stores or supermarkets, or make your own from sticks, string and paper.

Some kittens can be trained to retrieve a toy in much the same way as a dog will bring a ball back to his owner. The secret in training a cat to do anything is with a great deal of patience and a large supply of favourite food treats such as small pieces of chicken, fish or even cheese. Throw the toy for your kitten and, as soon as he brings it back to

It is fascinating to watch your kitten develop his hunting instincts as he plays.

The importance of grooming should not be underestimated – particularly if you have a longhair cat.

you, offer a food treat. Cats are ruled by their stomachs and will soon catch on to the idea that retrieving means food!

REGULAR GROOMING

Grooming is essential to keep the coat clean and untangled. It also helps to remove dead skin cells and improve circulation. While it is true that cats spend a great deal of time grooming themselves, they cannot reach everywhere and cannot check for health problems. Daily grooming also gives you an opportunity to build a closer relationship with your new kitten. The amount of time you need to spend on this will depend primarily on the length of your kitten's coat. Shorthair cats require a thorough grooming once a week, semi-longhairs need two or three sessions a week and longhair cats should be groomed every day. Try to keep to the same time each day, perhaps just before you feed him, so that grooming has positive associations.

It is never too early to start grooming your kitten, and, the more accustomed he is to this from an early age, the better. The secret to successful grooming is to make the whole experience as enjoyable for the cat as possible, so act confidently, keep calm and talk to him constantly, working for a maximum of 30 minutes at a time with frequent breaks. Do not try to physically restrain a struggling cat as you will always come off worst!

Before you start grooming,

gather everything you need together. Some items of equipment are essential, while others are simply nice to have. Your grooming equipment might include:

• Flea comb and metal comb (essential)
• Soft brush and slicker brush (essential)
• Piece of chamois leather or a grooming mitt (nice to have)
• Claw-clippers (nice to have if you are confident enough to use them)
• Small bowl filled with tepid water (essential)
• Cotton wool balls (essential)
• Baby oil (nice to have)
• Box of soft tissues (essential)
• Towel (essential)
• Tooth-cleaning products (essential)
• Round-ended scissors (nice to have)
• Unscented talcum powder (nice to have)

In warm weather you might like to groom your kitten outside so that the two of you can enjoy some sunshine. Sit the kitten on your knee and spend time stroking him until he is relaxed and happy. As you do this, you can examine

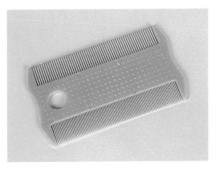

Flea comb.

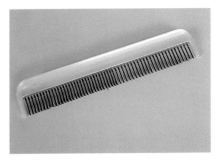

Metal comb.

Slicker brush.

Hold your kitten gently but firmly, and he will soon accept the grooming routine.

his teeth, eyes, ears and mouth for any evidence of discharge or bad smell which might require the vet's attention.

Check the claws but, if you are not confident about clipping them, ask your vet or a professional groomer to show you how, or to do it for you. Always use claw-clippers and cut straight across the white tip at the end of the claw. Never cut into the pink quick, as this causes bleeding and discomfort.

Trim away any long fur around the feet using a pair of round-ended scissors. This helps to keep the feet clean and tidy and prevents cat litter lodging between the toes.

GROOMING STEP-BY-STEP
Gently wipe each eye, using separate moist cotton wool balls, or cat eye-wipes to prevent infection and always wipe from the inside to the outside. Tear-staining can be removed with a commercial tear-stain remover or a warm, very weak saline solution.

One level teaspoonful of common salt per pint of water is sufficient.

Comb thoroughly, using a comb with wide-spaced teeth, particularly under the chin and other hard-to-reach areas. Remove any tangles and check for black specks which might indicate a problem with flea infestation.

Work your way from the head to the tail, combing the fur into sections and working on each section separately. Gently tease out any knots using your fingers.

Sprinkling longhair cats with talcum powder once a week will help you to brush out matts. There are also commercial dry shampoos available which do the same job.

Change to a slicker brush for longhairs, or a rubber brush or grooming mitt for shorthairs, to remove remaining dead hairs.

Your shorthair cat will benefit from having a few drops of conditioner or baby oil massaged into his coat once every few weeks. This will help remove grease and improve the shine and colour.

Give a final 'polish' using a chamois leather.

MOULTING

Outdoor cats generally moult in spring and autumn but indoor cats, living in centrally heated homes, can appear to be in a continual state of moult.

Hair-shedding is a natural process but very heavy hair loss at unexpected times can be a sign of illness. If you are concerned about this, contact your vet for advice.

From time to time a moulting cat may cough up or pass hair-balls. These consist of hair – ingested by the cat during grooming and collected in the stomach – which balls up into a tight mass. It can be quite alarming when your cat appears to be vomiting or retching in order to rid himself of these hair-balls, but he should only need the vet's attention if he appears very distressed, or has prolonged choking, or is extremely constipated.

The best way to minimise the formation of hair-balls, and to prevent the accumulation of loose hair on your furniture and clothes, is by regular grooming.

BATHING

Longhair cats will benefit from being bathed about once a month but it is rarely necessary to bathe a shorthair cat. Bathing should always be done after the cat has

This well-trained Persian kitten sits quietly, even when younger members of the family help with grooming.

been thoroughly combed, as any matts will 'set' when dry and be impossible to brush out.

Get everything you need ready first and, if you wash your cat in the sink or bath, place a rubber mat in the bottom to give your cat something to grip on to. The temperature of the water should be comfortable, neither too hot or too cold, but avoid getting water into the cat's eyes or ears.

A cat that is anxious about standing in water may accept standing on a dry surface and being rinsed with a hose, which is quieter and less powerful than a shower.

Always use proprietary cat shampoos and rinse off

thoroughly afterwards. Finish off by wrapping the cat in a thick towel and dry off the excess water. You may find it easier to ask a friend to help you by holding a hair-drier while you brush your cat.

TOOTH CARE

According to a survey on cat health by the University of Kansas in America, an amazing 85 per cent of cats over the age of three suffer from periodontal problems, with some cats developing problems at a much younger age.

Feeding a diet consisting of 70 per cent dry food and 30 per cent moist will help to reduce plaque and produce self-cleaning saliva. You can also accustom your young kitten to daily teeth

cleaning, which many of them find quite soothing and enjoyable. There are lots of cat dental care products on the market, including toothpaste and brushes or teeth-cleaning wipes, pads and solutions. Place a blob of cat toothpaste on your finger and let him sniff it, using one that he seems to like the taste of, and let him lick it before you begin. Now you can hold your cat from behind, under the chin, and gently rub the teeth using either a soft brush or your finger. Clean a couple of teeth the first few times and, as he accepts this, gradually do more.

It is recommended that a thorough check of the teeth is performed by a vet at least once a year.

5 *Health Matters*

To help ensure that your kitten grows into a healthy cat there are certain tasks you should perform routinely. Some are done on a daily basis, others are weekly, monthly or annually.

DAILY CHECKS

• Observe your kitten and be alert to any changes in his behaviour such as loss of appetite, excessive thirst, weight loss, unusual aggression or listlessness.

• Groom your kitten for a few minutes each day, especially if he is a longhair cat. This gives you the opportunity to check for obvious health problems such as fleas. As in humans, dull lifeless hair may indicate health problems.

• Check your kitten's teeth. Cleaning is not essential at a very young age because he will lose his baby teeth just before six months, but you can accustom him to having his mouth and gums handled. Heavy build-up of plaque on the teeth of adult cats can cause pain when eating and, possibly, the loss of teeth. This plaque can be removed under general anaesthetic by a vet, but feeding some dry food, or special anti-plaque chews, each day will help prevent build-up. Encourage him to tolerate daily tooth cleaning by trying some of the cat dental products available on the market.

• Dispose of any uneaten food the kitten leaves in his dish and thoroughly wash his food and water bowls.

• Remove any soiling from the litter tray.

WEEKLY CHECKS
• Check the eyes for signs of redness, discoloration or discharge. There should be no sign of the third eyelid.

• Check the ears. These are normally clean and pink, although slightly waxy. Look for evidence of discharge or a foul smell. Persistent scratching or head-shaking and excess wax may indicate ear mites, while a bad smell could be due to a bacterial or fungal infection.

• Check the nose and mouth. There should be no evidence of discharge or a foul smell.

• Soak the cat's litter tray using boiling water and disinfectant, avoiding strong-smelling products which may discourage the cat from using the tray. Alternatively, line the tray with a disposable litter tray liner which is thrown away with the dirty litter.

MONTHLY CHECKS
• Some methods of flea control are done on a monthly basis. (See separate section below for further details). Write the dates on a calendar to remind you.

• Outdoor cats that are keen hunters may benefit from a monthly regime of worm control. Indoor cats may only need this once or twice a year. Check with your vet for advice on worming.

ANNUAL CHECKS
• Your cat will require at least one trip to the vet each year for his vaccination boosters and annual health examination. Ask if your surgery sends out reminder letters and put a reminder in your diary to schedule an appointment.

• Book cattery dates well in advance, particularly if you holiday during the peak season.

• Check that your cat's health insurance is up to date.

VACCINATIONS
Vaccines provide protection against some of the most serious feline diseases including feline infectious enteritis, cat flu and feline leukaemia. **Feline Infectious Enteritis** is an extremely serious and often fatal

disease, producing many symptoms including dehydration, vomiting and diarrhoea. Routine vaccination has resulted in almost total control of this disease. **Cat Flu** is a common group of viral respiratory diseases which can make your kitten feel very ill but is rarely fatal. The vaccine protects against common strains of the viruses causing cat 'flu (i.e. feline herpes virus and feline calcivirus). **Feline Leukaemia** causes immunodeficiency disease and cancerous tumours in cats. It is very serious, and half the cats infected with this virus die of related diseases within two to three years. Vaccination gives a good degree of protection. There is now a combined vaccine available, which means one series of injections will cover your kitten against all three diseases, but check with your vet for further advice on the vaccinations he recommends.

Another virus worth mentioning is **Feline Immunodeficiency Virus** (FIV) sometimes referred to as the feline equivalent of the AIDS virus. This is NOT transmissible to humans and is not spread by sexual contact but primarily via cat bites. It is most prevalent among fighting tom cats and this is another major reason to have cats neutered. Scientists are working to develop an effective vaccine against FIV but, until this happens, neutering and isolation of infected cats is the best way to prevent the spread of FIV among the feline population.

Your kitten's first vaccinations are usually carried out between the ages of 8 and 12 weeks, when the antibodies he receives from his mother have dropped to a low enough level not to interfere with the vaccine. The usual recommendation is two doses of vaccine three to four weeks apart, followed by an annual booster. Reputable boarding catteries will ask you to produce vaccination certification from your vet, so do ensure that your cat's vaccinations are up to date five to six weeks before you board him.

PARASITE INFECTIONS

Cats can be infected by two groups of parasites – endoparasites that live inside the cat and ectoparasites that live on the surface of the cat. Examples of endoparasites include roundworms, tapeworms and lungworms. Examples of ectoparasites include fleas, ticks, lice and mites.

Worming products available on

the market are not preventative treatments, but they are curative, and will rid your cat of any parasites he or she may have picked up. They will not prevent re-infestation, so regular treatment is needed. Outdoor cats, particularly those who enjoy hunting, may be more prone to parasite infection than indoor cats. There are many worming preparations available, including some modern all-in-one types that require only one dose, although a separate course may be required for lungworm.

Flea infestation is the most common feline problem treated by vets. Fleas love the hospitality they find in the homes of cat owners, especially the warm, humid environment that central heating, double-glazing and fitted carpets provide. This means there is no longer a 'season' for fleas; they are found all year long.

Adult fleas are small, brownish-coloured insects, equipped with huge leg muscles enabling them to jump vast distances. They live in the coat of your cat and lay eggs which often drop to the ground and burrow into your carpet or soft furnishings until they are big enough to hatch and jump on to the nearest cat, dog or, as a last resort, human!

Tell-tale signs of fleas are small, black specks of dirt which fall off during grooming and are often visible if you comb your cat while he is standing on a clean white sheet of paper. Flea dirt contains congealed blood which will dilute to a pinkish colour if placed on a damp piece of cotton wool. Untreated flea infestation can be a severe source of skin irritation to your cat, causing itching and hair loss.

There are several new, safe and highly effective flea repellent products on the market but many are available only from your vet. Some products disrupt the breeding cycle of the flea by

rendering them infertile when they bite the cat. These are usually available as a liquid and are administered each month in the feed or in the form of an injection. Other preparations include collars, sprays, powders, foams or tablets. Check the labelling carefully as some older-style products may contain organophosphate ingredients and, if used, care should be taken with their administration and disposal. They are usually too strong for use on a kitten, or a cat who is nursing kittens.

Never use more than one product at a time on your cat and, if you suspect he or she has had an allergic reaction, contact your vet immediately.

Also available on the market is a range of 'alternative' flea repellents. These repellents differ from chemical insecticides in that they do not kill the flea and will not disrupt the flea's breeding cycle. They include flea repellent collars containing herbs and essential oils, shampoos or rinses, and applications of flea repellent oils such as lavender, rosemary, cedarwood or lemon diluted in a carrier oil.

Some owners have reported success by adding a quarter-teaspoonful of cider vinegar to the feed, which is supposed to make the cat's blood taste repugnant to fleas. Feeding garlic supplements is another popular method of natural flea control. For more information on natural health care products, contact your vet who will be able to advise you, as more and more vets have become interested in homeopathic remedies.

To prevent flea infestation:
• Comb your cat regularly with a special flea comb.
• If your cat is used to being bathed, try a flea repellent shampoo and rinse.
• Vacuum your home thoroughly and have the carpets steam-cleaned if infestation is suspected.
• Treat your cat's bedding and your home for flea infestation as well as the cat.

COMMON HEALTH PROBLEMS

Legend has it that cats have nine lives but, unfortunately, this does not mean you can ignore health problems in the hope that they will resolve themselves. By nature, cats are independent creatures, and often, when they are ill, will retreat to a quiet corner to lick their wounds rather than 'come to

mum' and tell you they have got a problem. This is why it is important for you to be vigilant with your cat, and to note his normal daily behaviour and appetite, so that you can spot sudden changes which may indicate a health problem.

Symptoms that should always be investigated by your vet include:
• Loss of appetite or excessive thirst.
• Sudden weight loss.
• Skin problems such as hair loss or sore patches.
• Persistent vomiting or diarrhoea.
• Discharge from the eyes or ears.
• Breathing problems.
• Abnormal behaviour such as hiding away or sudden aggression when touched.
• Lameness or inhibited movement.

In an emergency, such as a road accident, a cat will instinctively bolt and find somewhere to hide in an effort to avoid further injury and attack by predators. By the time injured cats are found, other symptoms have often developed such as dehydration, infection and/or shock. Telephone your veterinary surgery and alert them to the emergency. By law, each practice is obliged to offer a 24-hour emergency service but this may not be at the same premises, so do not waste time going to the wrong place. Transport the cat in a carrier or a strong cardboard box or restrain him in a towel.

Poisoning, accidental or otherwise, is a big problem for cats as they are less able to deal with the ingestion of toxic substances than other species. NEVER give your cat human medication unless directed by your vet. Aspirin and paracetamol can be highly toxic to cats and even one dose can be fatal.

Some cats, particularly white ones, are vulnerable to skin cancer. Like humans, cats should always have access to shade and cold water, but it may be worth applying a 'cat-safe' sun cream, based on titanium dioxide, to the tips of their ears and noses to help prevent sunburn. Unfortunately, most cats will lick creams off, so providing a shaded area is probably most helpful. Heatstroke is rare in cats with access to shade, but it can develop very quickly in cats who are left in a carrier in a stationery vehicle, so avoid this at all costs.

GIVING MEDICATION

Some cats are notoriously difficult to give medications to, and much patience is required. You can try mixing the medication with a favourite food, or hiding tablets in something the cat finds highly palatable, such as a prawn or piece

of chicken. This will help to mask the smell and taste of the medicine. Your vet will advise if you encounter severe problems.

COPING WITH CAT ALLERGIES

It can be very distressing to discover that a child or family member has an allergy to cats. Coughing, sneezing and runny eyes are just some of the uncomfortable symptoms that sufferers have to contend with, and some are so severe that they require medication such as antihistamines, or even steroids, to control them. People who suffer from asthma are also more likely to develop an adverse reaction to cats, and this is another factor to consider before getting your cat.

Some allergy sufferers react to cat dander, the skin particles routinely shed by cats, while others react to a substance which is secreted from the sebaceous glands of the cat's skin. Once these become airborne, they can be inhaled into the lungs or picked up on the skin, which develops into an allergic reaction.

Your GP will be able to provide specialist advice on treatments. This may include low-dosage desensitising techniques, which involve introducing minute samples of the allergen to the immune system at such low doses that the system no longer becomes compromised. The dose is gradually increased until the immune system can cope satisfactorily, but results are variable, and the technique is not suitable for all sufferers.

Fastidious house cleaning will help to relieve allergy symptoms, but do not vacuum immediately prior to a sufferer visiting as this only makes things worse by sending clouds of allergen into the air. Damp-dust regularly, wash curtains and soft furnishings and air the house thoroughly by opening the windows and ventilating the house. There are also various alternative medicine treatments available, such as homeopathic remedies or naturopathy.

6 *Understanding Your Kitten*

Animal behaviourists spend many hours studying the antics of kittens to try and understand what makes them tick. You too will enjoy spending time with your kitten, observing how he plays, hunts and communicates his needs. Most behaviour problems,

Close observation will help you to understand your cat's natural instincts and behaviour.

such as inappropriate spraying, are the result of stress and frustration at not getting their needs met, although most cats will try very persistently to make themselves understood. For example, any cat owner who has tried to ignore a hungry cat will report stories of how their cats try to attract attention by drastic means such as jumping on to their heads, sitting on the paperwork they are trying to work on, or even climbing on to shoulders and shouting in their owner's ear! Like us, cats vary in temperament and behaviour, but in the wild they are predatory creatures so, when they are frustrated in their attempt to get food, they increase their efforts in order to survive.

HOW CATS SEE

Because cats are hunters, their senses are highly tuned. Sunset and dawn are their most active times and cats' eyes are designed to give them optimum vision during these periods. You may notice occasionally, when your kitten is playing, that his eyes seem to become huge and, in fact, cats' pupils can open three times more than ours. In bright sunshine, however, the pupil shuts down to an almost horizontal slit and this gives them a much fuzzier image. Cats also have very effective night vision and it is thought they can see up to eight times better than us in the dark. Although they have effective vision, they see fewer colours than we do and cannot differentiate between reds, which probably look grey or black to them. They can make out shades of blue or green but are much more interested in the shape of an object, and its movement, than in its colour.

HOW CATS HEAR

Not only do cats see better than we do, they can hear much better too, especially those ultrasonic, high-pitched noises that are beyond our own range of hearing. They also have extremely sensitive pads on their feet, which come in handy when they are hunting, as they enable them to detect ground vibrations. Cats can tell from which direction a sound originates, using both ears to process the noise and then comparing the received information.

You will notice that your kitten will often put his head to one side when he is listening to

The cat has an acute sense of hearing.

something; this is his way of working out where a noise is coming from. He will do this less frequently as he grows older and more experienced. The ear flaps have a crinkled interior (referred to by vets as the external ear or pinna). The crinkles keep the pinna rigid, but they also introduce minute distortions into the sounds passing into the middle ear and so help the cat to recognise the height of a sound.

HOW CATS COMMUNICATE

Your kitten has many methods of communication but, to us humans, purring is certainly one of the nicest. There can be few things more relaxing than sitting quietly with a purring kitten on your knee and there is scientific evidence to prove that this activity can actually help lower our blood pressure. Not everything is known about purring but it is thought that the sound is produced by the cat's vocal cords vibrating together. The glottis (the gap between the chords) opens and closes up to 25 times per second and the pressure of air passing in and out results in the noise we recognise as purring. Purring occurs when the cat is happy and relaxed, and it is often used in greeting and accompanied by rolling, or rubbing against a familiar person.

Purring can also occur when a cat is distressed or worried, such as during a visit to the vet. In this case purring is thought to be a source of comfort and a plea for help from other cats or from their owner. It probably relates back to happier times when the kitten was snuggled up with his purring mother.

COMMON BEHAVIOURAL PROBLEMS

Observing and understanding your cat's natural behaviour will help you to encourage behaviours you enjoy, such as gentle play, and discourage unwanted behaviour, such as aggression. If any sudden behaviour changes develop, take the cat for a thorough examination by the vet to rule out physical causes.

Purring is a sign that your cat is happy, relaxed, and content.

The aim is to encourage the behaviour you want, and to gently discourage undesirable behaviour.

INDOOR SPRAYING AND SOILING

Indoor spraying accounts for up to 65 per cent of the problems encountered by animal behaviourists and, having first ruled out a medical problem, the next step is to determine whether the cat is spraying or soiling to mark out his territory, or whether there is another unexplained reason. It is not always known to owners when a new cat has moved into the neighbourhood, but territory marking can often develop when this happens. It may also occur when the cat's security is challenged by some disruption to his routine within the home, such as building work or decorating. A cat that is marking often sprays in these areas but still continues to use the litter tray. On the other hand, cats with toileting problems often stop using the litter tray completely, preferring to use a quiet, secluded place such as behind a sofa or under a bed! Refusal to use the litter tray is often a first sign of inappropriate toileting problems.

Kittens who experience problems with house training may have been set a poor example by their mothers, or may not have been provided with a litter tray close to the nest. They may also be used to one type of cat litter and disapprove of the one you have provided, so check with the breeder or cattery and find out what kind of cat litter was used so that you can get a supply. You may also find that changing the position of the litter tray will resolve the problem. Your cat may reject it because it is in a high traffic area such as a busy hallway, or if it has been placed too close to his food bowls. The frequency and zeal with which you clean the litter tray can also affect the

Patience is essential when dealing with any type of behavioural problem.

success of house training. If you are over-zealous with cleaning you may be removing all traces of the smell of urine and this may discourage the cat from using the tray. On the other hand, some cats will reject a tray that is left dirty for too long.

Fastidious cleaning of a soiled area is an essential element of treatment, but never use a cleaner that contains ammonia and/or chlorine as these are also constituents of cat urine and can confuse the cat even more. Wash the area with a warm solution of biological detergent and, when it is dry, scrub thoroughly with surgical spirit (remember to perform a fabric test first). Next, place a bowl of dried cat food over the cleaned area, as this helps reinforce to the cat that the area is a feeding place and will deter future soiling.

Cats who do not respond to simple changes in housekeeping, such as repositioning the litter tray, changing litter type and thorough cleaning of soiled areas, may benefit from going back to basics. An animal behaviourist may recommend confining the cat to a pen, or a small room, containing only a bed and a litter tray, for a few days. This limits the choices of where the cat should soil and the urge not to soil in his bed will help him choose the litter tray. Confinement in this way should never be long-term – a couple of days will be sufficient.

Never resort to physical abuse when dealing with house training or any other behaviour problems. Remember, the cat has very good reasons of his own for soiling or spraying where he does. Urine spraying is normal feline behaviour and exhibited naturally by all outdoor cats. It simply becomes unacceptable to us when the cat performs the behaviour indoors.

Finding out why the cat needs to spray or soil indoors is the first step to resolving the problem and a qualified animal behaviourist will help you do this and develop a successful treatment programme. Physical abuse will only make the problem worse, as does chasing the cat, or waving your arms and shouting, all of which he may find quite entertaining. Contact your vet for details of a counsellor in your area.

HATRED OF GROOMING

As with anything else, prevention is better than cure when it comes to grooming problems. Start

Cats that have been brought up together rarely become aggressive, but, occasionally, relations break down.

grooming your new kitten immediately, especially if he is longhaired. Adverse reactions usually occur as a result of pain, such as someone being rough when removing matts from his coat. Have your cat checked over by a vet to ensure that he has not got a medical problem such as skin irritation, or an abscess developing, which will account for his dislike of grooming. When he has been given the all-clear, resolve to make the grooming experience as pleasant as possible. Be prepared to adopt a very patient approach. Begin by, literally, just laying a brush on the cat's coat, then quickly removing it and giving the cat a food treat as a reward. Breaking the grooming down into small components will help. Begin by getting the cat to accept sitting on your knee, or wherever you want to groom him, and do not put pressure on him by grooming for too long at any one session. A few minutes of successful grooming is better than an hour-long session resulting in the cat becoming angry and aggressive.

REFUSING THE CAT CARRIER

Some owners complain that, on the rare occasions they get the carrier out to take their cat to the vet or cattery, the cat disappears for hours on end. The answer to this problem is to make sure that the carrier becomes a routine part of the cat's everyday life and is not associated with unpleasant events. Take the carrier out of storage and leave it out in the open near the cat's bed. Put some toys and food treats inside it and encourage your kitten to explore by himself. Your cat will soon realise the carrier is not threatening and, with time, will go inside quite happily.

AGGRESSION

Cats who are in pain can suddenly develop aggressive behaviour, so it is vital that you take them to the vet for a thorough examination. If no medical cause is found, then the cause of the aggression may be rooted in a fear response. A detailed review of the cat's environment, recent history and long-term lifestyle should be undertaken. Perhaps a new cat has moved into the neighbourhood or there has been disruption in the household such as divorce or even a wedding. It can be very upsetting for owners to experience aggression from their cats, but a visit to an animal behaviourist will help you get to the root cause of the problem and develop a treatment programme to overcome this.

Equally upsetting to owners is when cats who have lived together in harmony for several years apparently fall out and become aggressive towards each other. Often the reason for a rift between cats is a subtle change in the cat's scent, perhaps because of a trip to the vet, cattery or a show. Resist the temptation to shout at the aggressive cat and rush to protect the 'victim' as this will only perpetuate the aggressive cat's opinion that his former best friend is now his worst enemy. Instead, try feeding the aggressive cat, or giving him a treat when the other cat is present, so that pleasant associations being to re-establish themselves.

In extreme cases, you may have to reintroduce the cats to each other as if they were strangers. This is achieved by getting them to accept each other's scent. Keep the cats separate and provide each one with a towel or an old jumper to sleep on. Every night alternate the towels so that they get used to each other's scent. After a couple of weeks reintroduce the cats by confining one of them to an indoor pen and allowing them to sniff each other in safety. Next day, reverse the situation by allowing the confined cat freedom to roam and confining the other one, then introduce them again. With patience and time, the cats should, once again, begin to accept each other, but there are no guarantees, and, if the falling out is very severe, it may be necessary to consider re-homing one of the cats or to keep them permanently separated.

DESTRUCTIVE BEHAVIOUR

Cats can cause a great deal of damage with their claws, particularly to furniture and wallpaper. They can also cause damage within the home by breaking ornaments or by chewing and scratching a favourite rug. It is important to

Providing toys and scratching posts will curb tendencies towards destructive behaviour.

realise that cats are never motivated by malice towards their owners – even if they have had a particularly bad day they will never think "I am going to knock this china teapot on the floor and really annoy someone". They are simply amusing themselves.

Scratching is also normal cat behaviour and is essential for several reasons, including removing outer claw sheaths, claw-conditioning and providing visual and scent signals to other cats. If you keep your cat permanently indoors, it is vital that you provide him with a scratching post to allow him to perform this behaviour in a place that is acceptable to you. Introducing a new kitten to the scratching post at an early age will help prevent problems from developing.

Scratching as a means of scent marking can be deterred by thorough cleaning of the area with biological washing powder and surgical spirit to remove all traces of the scent. Never ignore destructive feline behaviour, even in tiny kittens, as it can develop into a compulsive disorder. Try to distract your kitten from developing a preoccupation with the wallpaper or furniture by

playing another game with him. In addition, keep a plastic water spray bottle handy and spray the cat, while saying a loud "No", if you catch the cat scratching wallpaper or furniture. A well-aimed jet of water reinforces the message that scratching in this area is unacceptable. Immediately take the cat to his scratching post so that he knows where he can exercise his claws. As with all persistent behaviour problems, contact a qualified pet behaviour counsellor if the problem continues.

HUNTING
Cats are natural hunters and often enjoy bestowing special people, particularly their owners, with a gift such as a mouse or a dead bird. Unfortunately, these gifts are not always appreciated by their owners who tend to scream and make a fuss, causing the cat much confusion! It is far more effective to ignore the cat and attempt to distract him from his prey using food or a toy. Putting a collar with a bell on the cat may help alert birds and other animals that your cat is on the warpath and there is some evidence that red collars are the most visible to birds. Unfortunately, cats can

The cat is a natural hunter – and although you can limit his opportunities, you will not alter his mind-set.

become very adept at moving so slowly that the bell does not make a noise until it is too late. Keeping your cat indoors at those prime hunting times, the early morning and at dusk, will help preserve wildlife in your area. If you put food out for birds, then place it in a wide open space to give the birds an escape route and to prevent your cat from reaching them too easily.

7 Growing Up

Your kitten will quickly establish himself as a member of your family and soon you will forget what life was like before he arrived. Time can pass so quickly that, before you know it, your kitten has reached the age of six months which, for female kittens, is the onset of sexual maturity. From this age, your female kitten can become pregnant and produce up to three litters a year, with five or six kittens in each litter. Your little male cat is capable of fathering a litter at seven months. It is vital, therefore, that you arrange to have your kitten neutered as soon as he or she is old enough.

THE IMPORTANCE OF NEUTERING

It is an old wife's tale that females should be allowed to have one litter before they are spayed. On the contrary, there is some evidence that mammary cancer is more common in cats that have had kittens. Even if you find homes for all the kittens your cat has, you will not know what will happen to those kittens who may in themselves go on to be responsible for producing over 20,000 descendants!

Another advantage of neutering is that cats often become much more affectionate towards their owners and are less likely to become involved in fights and pick up a virus such as FIV or Feline Leukaemia. They are also much less likely to stray or mark their territory by indoor urine spraying. If your kitten has been adopted from a Cats Protection League centre you will be expected to agree to your kitten being neutered and will be handed a neutering certificate at the time of adoption. This should be signed by your vet at the time of surgery and returned to the CPL so they can maintain their records.

Female cats should be spayed from six months and your vet will advise you about this. A short stay at the surgery will be required, followed by a second visit a week later to remove stitches. Male cats should be castrated at six months, which involves a very simple, routine operation under anaesthetic with a brief stay at the surgery. The cost of surgery will vary, so check this beforehand and enquire about payment options if you think you will have difficulty in paying. Some animal charities provide neutering at a reduced cost for owners in financial difficulties.

In no time, your tiny kitten will start to mature, and you must take on board his changing needs.

Your cat is a much-loved member of the family, so take great care when making arrangements for others to care for him.

CHOOSING A CATTERY

There are times when you may need to board your kitten at a cattery. Ask other cat owners which cattery they recommend and pay a visit to the premises. Alternatively, write to the Feline Advisory Bureau, the internationally-known, British-based charity dedicated to the health and welfare of cats, and ask for a list of approved FAB catteries in your area. The charity also has a web site. Reputable catteries always welcome visitors and, provided you do not arrive at

a busy time of the day, will be happy to show you round prior to your cat boarding. Check for the following:

• Is everywhere spotlessly clean?
• Are the chalets big enough? They should be at least four feet square and have a sneeze barrier of about two feet between pens to reduce the risk of infection passing from one cat to another.
• Are the chalets well insulated, clean and painted? Is there adequate ventilation and heating?
• Do the cats look clean and well cared for? Are their litter trays

clean? What type of bedding is used? Can you take your own?

• Are you asked to produce vaccination certificates? Does the proprietor ask for your cat's feeding history, vet's name and contact telephone numbers?

• Is fresh water available in all the pens?

• Do the chalets have locking cat flaps?

• Where is the food prepared? Does the kitchen area look clean and well organised?

• Does the price include everything or are there extra costs for heating?

• Will your cat be groomed?

• What will happen if your cat is ill during his stay?

• How much are cancellation fees and what insurance arrangements does the cattery have?

Make an early reservation to get into a good cattery as they become booked up very early, especially during peak periods such as Christmas, Easter and school holidays. Ensure that you know the times you can arrive with your cat and pick him up again. Telephone immediately if you experience delays and will be late picking your cat up, or you may face extra fees.

CARING FOR OLDER CATS

Thanks to significant advances in feline nutrition, medicine and health care, cats are living longer than ever, and many cats survive to at least the age of 15, with some living much longer. As your cat approaches middle-age, he will gradually become less active and his metabolism will slow down. You may notice that he sleeps more than he used to. As with humans, this is an age when cats are vulnerable to middle-age spread and may need light or diet food to prevent them from becoming obese. Regularly weighing your cat throughout his life will help you to keep an eye on any changes. Do this by weighing yourself on the bathroom scales and then repeat the process holding the cat in your arms. Then subtract the cat's weight from your own. It is important to note significant weight loss as well as weight gain.

Older cats can become fussy about what they will eat. If this happens, ensure your vet checks your cat's teeth to rule out dental problems as a cause. Older cats will benefit from a six-monthly check-up, or more frequently if necessary.

The older cat deserves special consideration.

Your aged cat may also be prone to kidney problems and could benefit from eating more wet food with a higher water content which may be easier for him to digest. Signs of kidney problems can include excessive thirst and weight loss. Your vet may prescribe medication to help the kidneys function correctly and relieve the symptoms.

Providing your cat with a bean bag rather than a standard bed will ensure he is comfortable in his old age and it will offer extra support. Heated beds are available on the market, but placing an ordinary bed next to a radiator and well away from draughts should be sufficient.

If your older cat still likes to go outdoors, make sure you dry him off thoroughly if he returns wet and cold. Many owners report a tendency for their older cats to flatly refuse to go out during winter and so you may need to provide him with a litter tray. Similarly, he may experience difficulties with mobility and a carefully positioned stool or chair will help him jump on to surfaces such as a favourite windowsill where he can enjoy the feel of sunshine on his back.

Cats who previously were very adept at grooming themselves may need a little more help in old age. Stiffness and lack of mobility may mean they are not as able to turn and reach those awkward places.

As they are less active, they may also need regular claw-clipping, which your vet will be happy to do for you if you are not confident about doing this. By being vigilant and adaptable you will ensure that your cat copes well with old age.

SAYING GOODBYE

Part of the responsibility of caring for your cat means making the difficult decision to have him put to sleep if and when he becomes too ill to enjoy a meaningful quality of life.

Your vet will help and advise you when the time comes to say goodbye but you can be reassured by the fact that it will be done very quickly and sympathetically, either at the surgery or in your own home. Every care is taken to ensure that the cat does not become distressed and, if necessary, a sedative is given first to keep him really calm and peaceful. Your vet will then carefully inject the cat with an overdose of anaesthetic.

Many owners choose to bury their cat in the garden but your vet will take the cat away with him if you prefer. You may also consider using the services of a pet crematorium.

Some owners are comforted by remembering their cat with a permanent reminder such as planting a plaque or rosebush in his favourite place in the garden, or commissioning a painting from a photograph.

Perhaps, however, the greatest comfort to any grieving owner is the knowledge that they have done the best for their cat throughout his life and helped to provide him with a dignified and peaceful end to his old age.

There is also some evidence that cats from multi-cat households go through their own grieving process at the loss of a companion, so try and offer them lots of reassurance and

When the end comes, try to remember all the happy times you have spent together.

attention to help compensate for their loss.

Never be afraid to ask for help if you feel you are not coping well with your grief. Many vet's surgeries offer bereavement counselling to owners who are overwhelmed by the emotions they experience.

Gradually, as the weeks and months pass following the death of your cat, happy thoughts of your lives together will begin to ease your sorrow. In the meantime, cherish every moment you have together and enjoy the many years and fun that owning a kitten will bring you!